MAGNA BOOKS

ROLLING STONES
IMAGES OF THE WORLD TOUR 1989 - 1990

ROLLING STONES
IMAGES OF THE WORLD TOUR 1989 - 1990
Text by David Fricke and Robert Sandall
Additional text by Rod Green

This edition Published in 1995
by MAGNA BOOKS, Magna Road, Wigston,
Leicester LE18 4ZH, UK.

First published in the UK 1990
by BOXTREE LIMITED, Broadwall House, 21 Broadwall, London SE1 9PL

Copyright: ©1990 Musidor B.V.
Europe section of text © Robert Sandall 1990
USA section of text © David Fricke 1990
Other text © Boxtree Ltd. 1990

All Rights reserved

ISBN 1 85422 877 3

12345678910
Art and design direction: Mick Jagger, Charlie Watts, Lance Yates
Compiled by Tony King, Jane Rose, Lance Yates
Design by: Dave Crook
Edition Rod Green
Photographers: Eugene Adebari, Mikio Agriga, George Chin, Claude Gassian,
          Kevin Mazur, Paul Natkin, Dimo Safari, Albert Watson

Front Cover Photograph: Albert Watson

Printed in Italy by New Interlitho, Milan

A CIP catalogue record for this book is available from the British Library

INTRODUCTION

They were alive, but were they kicking? Today, with the benefit of 15 months worth of hindsight and 115 packed out stadium shows in North America, Europe and Japan as hard evidence, the question sounds merely facetious. Back in early 1989, however, the outcome of what soon turned into the biggest, best attended and quite simply the best rock and roll tour ever, looked a lot less certain. The Stones hadn't ventured out on the road for 7 years, the longest such gap in their entire career. In the interim there had been births, marriages and solo careers to preoccupy individual band members, as well as one tragic death which, far more even than all the mischievous rumourmongering of the world's gutter press, had seriously threatened band unity for the first time. On December 12, 1985, the "sixth Stone", Ian Stewart, died of a heart attack. With his abrupt departure the group lost a founder member, a great piano player and a close friend whose comparative immunity to all the alienating rigmaroles of stardom had helped to keep everybody's mind on the job. Without "Stu", the famous five's unique cohesiveness was suddenly put at risk. And, what with one thing and another, by the time plans for Steel Wheels ground into motion 3 years later, the Stones weren't just winding up for another album with triumphal tour attached. In the public perception at least, they were attempting the most difficult move in the game. The Rolling Stones were making a comeback.

That they pulled it off so confidently was, in the event, only partly down to the enduring potency of the myth of "the greatest rock and roll band in the world". Sure, we all re-discovered the truth that some of those songs just will not grow old. Sure, the Stones proved yet again that they could pull in as many youthful "first timers" as they could returning regulars. But what held them there, in record numbers (over 6 million) this time, had a lot to do with the band's unprecedented attention to the fine detail of their performance on the one hand, and to a clear sighted vision of how to stage a show in a stadium on the other. The Stones managed to look enormous without sounding pompous or monumental. They were impressive and expressive at the same time. Here was a massively entertaining, grand spectacle which never neglected the intimacies and intricacies of the music that kick started everything in the first place. The person who came up with that line, "Think global, act local" must have been waiting for this tour to come to town.

Now, though, there is another question: will they, or when will they, be back? Nobody, of course, is saying anything very definite on this point. Jagger and Richards will point out that they have continuing solo interests; on the domestic front, wives and families claim more of everybody's attention these days. And you simply can't make a regular habit of leaving home and living out of suitcases for as long as this adventure lasted when time isn't quite on your side the way it used to be. But the smart money says that the Stones will hit the road again at some point, and for two very simple reasons. They still love what they do, and they are still very, very good at it.

Never been better, in fact.

Robert Sandall

MONTSERRAT

There were no guarantees when it all started. Having stowed their emotional baggage about the long-term future of the Rolling Stones (and their own personal relationship) in a dark corner somewhere, Mick Jagger and Keith Richards agreed to have another go at songwriting together in January, 1989. "I just ignored all that crap," Jagger said later, dismissing the battle of wills and wits which had escalated in the years after *Dirty Work*. "I thought we should just get on with it. You know, English people are like that. They carry on. Stiff upper lip."

For the next two months, at Eddy Grant's studio on the Caribbean island of Barbados, Jagger and Richards applied that stoical resolve to the job at hand with spectacular results. By quitting time in late February, there were 12 new songs bearing the Jagger/Richards brand, not to mention 40 or so leftovers - mostly unfinished melodies, riffs and lyrics - on the cutting room floor.

The productivity rate alone was impressive, but there was also a kick and class to the new material that had been lacking in recent Stones albums. On records like *Emotional Rescue* and *Tattoo You*, Jagger and Richards mostly fashioned new tunes from old, tarted-up outtakes or skeletal jam ideas. This time they started from scratch, realigning the intuitive creative balance that yielded some of their greatest triumphs - *Beggars Banquet, Let It Bleed, Sticky Fingers, Exile On Main Street*. They came up trumps.

The future singles *Mixed Emotions* and *Rock And A Hard Place* bristled with the refined primitivism of the band's best early seventies work. The bittersweet ache of *Almost Hear You Sigh* and *Slipping Away* showed that Jagger and Richards had not lost their ballad touch. For *Continental Drift* they even detoured back to the eastern modal investigations of *Paint It Black*.

Their enthusiasm proved contagious. When the full band convened at George Martin's AIR Studios in Montserrat to commence work on *Steel Wheels*, they played like they were training for a championship fight, cutting tracks and jamming for up to fifteen hours at a stretch. At one point in the sessions, Bill Wyman took a trip to nearby Antigua to fend off British tabloid snoops sniffing around for news on his impending wedding to Mandy Smith. While he was off hosting a press conference, the other Stones cranked out four tunes with Ron Wood on bass.

With Chris Kimsey (a veteran of Stones sessions since 1971) co-producing, the band cut the basic tracks for the album in only five weeks, recording everything live in the studio.

"This music, it's certainly not Beethoven or Mozart," Richards said with evident delight during the mixing sessions later in London. "It's got nothing to do with intricacy. It's got to do with a bunch of guys making accidents together, spontaneity and an immediate form of communication."

Just like old times.

Sheik Jagger jams with the Master Musicians of Jajouka.

MOROCCO

The flight from London took only a couple of hours, but the time change was something else again. In mid-June, Mick Jagger and Keith Richards set off for a weekend of recording and serious *deja vu* in Morocco, where they had vacationed in the late sixties and where the late Brian Jones, had discovered the mystical 4000-year-old sounds of the Master Musicians of Jajouka. As the Tangier sun poured into a 16th century palace courtyard inside the historic Kasbah, Jagger (dressed like the Sheik of Shake in an elegant white kaftan) and Richards - joined by Ron Wood, who dashed in for the weekend as well - let the tapes roll and basked in the primal glow of the Master Musicians' joyous, untamed noise, the influence of which was eventually felt in *Continental Drift*.

CONNECTICUT

They didn't even say hello. They didn't have to. The staccato bark of Keith Richards' guitar at the beginning of *Start Me Up* said it all as the Stones launched their fall Steel Wheels sortie with an unannounced barroom warmup on August 12th at Toad's Place. In this 700–capacity club in New Haven, Connecticut, the Stones blitzed a packed house of delirious and very surprised fans with a searing fifty–minute set that augured well for the stadium spectaculars to come.

It was an evening of sweat, smiles and swinging from the rafters, of relishing the sexual thrust and banshee scream of rock & roll in its native garage and barroom environment. Unsuspecting fans had paid a paltry $3.01 to get in, expecting just another Saturday night dance party. The opening act, a local combo called Sons of Bob, didn't realise they were *hors d'oeuvres* for the Stones until the band's gear arrived.

Secret pre–tour club shows were nothing new to the Stones; the '81 U.S. tour was prefaced by a riotous gig – with the emphasis on 'riot' – at a club in Worcester, Massachusetts which was beseiged by angry fans who couldn't get in. At Toad's Place, though, the fireworks were all indoors as the

Stones, assisted by Leavell and Clifford at the ivories, ripped through *Miss You, It's Only Rock 'n' roll* and *Brown Sugar* with vintage verve. *Sad, Sad, Sad,* and *Mixed Emotions* from the as yet unreleased *Steel Wheels* made their stage debuts and halfway through the set the band dropped down into a lean, mean version of Willie Dixon's *Little Red Rooster* - a relic from their purist R&B days – that would later be a highlight of the outdoor shows.

The Toad's Place rave–up was a kind of Graduation Day party for the Stones, marking the end of a seven–week residency in suburban Connecticut packed solid with intensive rehearsals, tour production meetings and promotional activities for the new album. It had already been a work intensive year for the band. Steel Wheels was written, recorded and mixed in a dizzying six months – record time for a band that, in recent, years, had regularly taken thrice that to make an album. Yet within a week of tidying up the final mixes at Olympic Studios in London, the Stones and their entourage had set up camp in the rural hamlet of Washington, Connecticut. The local population swelled overnight with the band's families, friends, business

A ghetto blaster gave the press a taste of *Mixed Emotions*.
The *Mixed Emotions* video was recorded during rehearsals in Connecticut. (left and opposite right)

associates and tour personnel while the Stones commandeered Wykeham Rise, a former girls' boarding school, as a practise space.

And practise they did. "We just shut the door and played," recalled ex–Allman Brothers pianist Chuck Leavell, who divided up keyboard duties with young British sessioneer Matt Clifford. The Stones' original "wish" list for the show ran to 75 songs – which would have made the show about six hours long. That was eventually pared down by more than half, to a more manageable 28 songs, with a few numbers popping in and out of the set as the tour progressed. *Play With Fire* was replaced in the ballad spot by *Angie* in mid–route; *Shattered* was dropped after the first night in Philadelphia; *Salt Of The Earth*, a rarely aired gem from *Beggar's Banquet*, would be dusted off for the big end–of–tour blow out in Atlantic City.

On July 11th, the Stones took the day off for a trip to New York City, where they played host to the world's press with characteristic flamboyance. After letting 450 international newshounds bake in near–hundred degrees heat for about an hour in an

American choreographer Lavelle Smith puts Mick through his paces.

un–air–conditioned waiting room at Grand Central Station, the band pulled into track 42 aboard a chartered commuter train, riding in a Roaring Twenties–style caboose which had been featured in Francis Ford Coppola's film, *The Cotton Club*. Jagger made a short, perfunctory speech about the *Steel Wheels* tour and album, gave the press a tantalizing taste of *Mixed Emotions* on a little boom box and, with Richards, verbally deflected the generally hapless questions with practiced *hauteur*.

Q: "Some rock critics have charged that the only reason you're doing it is for the money."

Jagger: "What about love and fame and fortune? Have you forgotten about all those things?"

To which Keith Richards added with impish glee, "The glory, darlin', the glory!"

With Connecticut reeling in their wake, the Stones decamped for Long Island where they set up shop at Nassau Coliseum for dress rehearsals with the complete "industrial holocaust" stage set and full lights 'n' pyro. In less than three weeks it would be opening night and the feast of glory would begin.

START ME UP

After seven years off the road, the
Rolling Stones weren't about to just
walk on stage each night and say "Hi,
(your city here), did you miss us?" As
it was on the '81-'82 tour, *Start Me Up* -
an *Emotional Rescue* outtake later
hammered into shape for *Tattoo You* -
was the opening salvo. This time
around, though, the Stones
transformed the song into a declaration
of war, prefacing the metallic cackle of
Keith Richards' opening riff with a
nuclear chorus of fireworks and a wall
of fire three hundred feet across.
When the smoke cleared, Richards had
dropped down into his fighting crouch,
choking the neck of his Telecaster with
undisguised vigour. Ron Wood,
cigarette dangling precipitously from
his pursed lips, sprayed the crowd
with bluesy shards of steely guitar.
And Mick Jagger - no doubt piqued by
charges that he veered dangerously
close to self-parody on the last tour -
was in firm command of centre stage,
eschewing excessive sexual camp for
the leonine cool of a veteran road
warrior. With the Watts 'n' Wyman
backfield maintaining rhythm order
with their usual aplomb, it was more
than enough, as the song goes, to
make a grown man, or woman, cry -
for joy.

STEEL WHEELS

The Rolling Stones had just whipped nearly 55,000 people at Veterans Stadium in Philadelphia into a roaring frenzy with a double welcoming whammy of *Start Me Up* and *Bitch*, and were mid-way through a steaming *Shattered* when the sound system - all 550,000 watts of it - went stone dead. After a year of planning, months of preparation and no expense spared, a single generator fault brought the Stones Steel Wheels juggernaut grinding to a brief, but nonetheless embarrassing, halt. On the opening night.

It took the engineers just three minutes to locate and rectify the problem - the only major bummer of the entire fourteen week North American tour. Knowing a bad omen when they saw it, the Stones dropped *Shattered* from the set list after the August 30th opening show and got down to the business of putting on the best single-act stadium show in the history of rock and roll.

The Stones, of course, invented the modern rock concert. Tightly choreographed package tours and breathless half-hour headline sets rendered inaudible by screaming teenage girls were still a fresh, rather unpleasant memory for the band

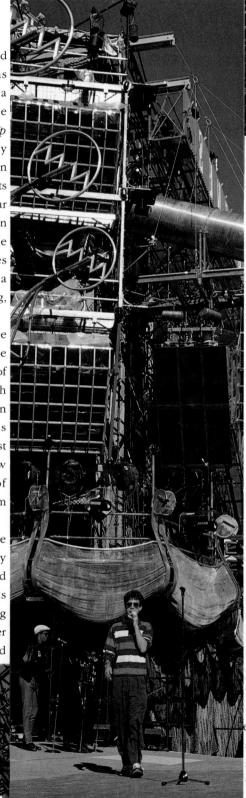

when they embarked on their legendary 1969 American comeback trek. This time around, the show was the thing. The World's Greatest Rock and Roll Band strutted their incomparable stuff in the nation's biggest arenas, transforming soulless stadia into Dionysian ballrooms - at least for the evening - and setting a major precedent for the presentation of live rock.

For the Steel Wheels tour, the Stones reinvented the concert experience all over again. Returning to the outdoor mega-stadia which had been their home-on-the-road since the 1978 Some Girls tour, they performed not on a mere stage, but in a travelling futureshock environment - part *Blade Runner* fantasy, part grim urban reality - which set designer Mark Fischer described as guerilla architecture. Eight storeys high and wider than a football pitch, the set was the largest transportable rock concert structure ever built, a skyscraping Frankenstein aggregate of pipes, girders, chutes, catwalks, mock radio towers and cracked satellite dishes. In the daylight hours it looked like everyone's worst nuclear nightmare, an awesome mess of metallic chaos and ersatz industrial rot. After sunset, when the Stones came on, it took on the menacing, all-too-real aura of the oil and chemical refineries belching

Guns 'N' roses supported the Stones in Los Angeles and the Gunners'lead singer, W. Axl Rose, flew into Atlantic City to join Mick on stage.

Award winning band Living Colour filled the regular support slot on the Steel Wheels tour. Living Colour's 1988 debut album, *Vivid*, sold over two million copies worldwide, paving the way for their follow–up, *Time's Up*. They were voted "Best New American Band" in the '89 Rolling Stone Readers' Poll.

deathsmoke along the New Jersey Turnpike.

The basic design arithmetic was apocalyptic itself. It took as many as 120 people around a week to erect the stages; that's right, there were two of them, leapfrogging from stadium to stadium. The radio towers rose so far above the scaffolding, topping off at 130 feet, that federal law required the installation of blinking red aircraft collision lights (which made the whole thing look even more authentic). The show's entire pyro package - including the big bang finale, accompanied by Bizet's *March of the Toreadors* - featured nearly 50,000 fireworks and 100,000 pounds of aerial shells, not to mention a ton of flash powder.

But instead of being dwarfed by the physical immensity of the stage and its dramatic air of rack and ruin, the Stones reigned over it all like kings of the slum, celebrating their own weather-beaten durability and indomitable spirit with hardened muscle and outlaw vigour. "It had to reflect the Rolling Stones story in 1989," lighting designer Patrick Woodroffe said of the Steel Wheels spectacle in one interview. "It had to have dignity. It had to be tough, hard and current rather than nostalgic and beautiful."

Like the music itself the Stones had everything to prove, and lose, by their nightly stage raids. After so long off the road and a less-than-lustrous mid-eighties studio streak, the Stones were competing not only with their spiritual offspring dogging them on the charts (Guns 'N' Roses et al.) but with their own daunting legacy.

Nothing less than their integrity and continuing relevance were at stake.

That they still like-nothing better than a good kick up the caboose before going on was apparent in their choice of opening act, the killer black rock band Living Colour. Jagger had been instrumental in getting the group a record deal, producing two demos for them in '87, and he knew what they were capable of; raging psycho-funk, smouldering blues and hurricane thrash, all charged with the racial pride and soul-fire that had been the hallmark of the Stones' great opening acts through the years - Ike and Tina Turner, B. B. King, Stevie Wonder, The Meters, Prince.

For their four night run at the Memorial Coliseum in Los Angeles, the Stones even upped the ante by booking LA premier badasses Guns 'N' Roses as special guests. With all due respect to the Gunners, who certainly wowed their friends and neighbours, it was "like putting a Honda scooter on a highway with a Harley", as one critic put it in the Village Voice. The Stones had age, experience, tunes and undiminished insolence on their side. And they came by their attitude naturally - they were born with it.

Richards sounded reveille every night with the familiar

Tele stutter of *Start Me Up*, but it was Jagger - first appearing in white shirt , tight black pants and Napoleonesque green tails - who set the tone of the evening. He wailed with lusty strength and unmistakable commitment. The nervous agitation in his trademark sexual karate belied the practised grace and dynamic exaggeration with which he worked the stage and played to the cameras broadcasting his every manoeuvre on the giant video screens. He made the most of the latter especially during *2000 Light Years From Home*, when his slow-mo shadow dancing was set against a "vintage" sixties oil-bubble light show.

After so long it's easy to take the Stones' greatest strengths for granted - the slash and snarl of Keef and Woody's guitar crossfire, the bedrock rhythms of Bill Wyman and Charlie Watts, the harsh argumentative lyricism with which Jagger and Richards have documented the high costs and tainted rewards of bedroom politics and emotional warfare. But *One Hit (To The Body)*, a *Dirty Work* number new to the live repertoire, was a brilliantly rude awakening, riveting in its frank brutality. The taut, torrid version of *Gimme Shelter* - capping an epic suite featuring *Paint It Black, 2000 Light Years From Home* and *Sympathy For The Devil* - was shot through with Altamont horror and Crack City paranoia. Jagger's

rousing duet with backing singer Lisa Fischer, who sang like one of Hells Belles, was a chilling highlight of every show.

The North American leg of the Rolling Stones world tour came to a suitably impressive climax on December 20th with a radio and cable TV simulcast of the final show at the Atlantic City Convention Center, where the band played to a bizarre mix of hardcore fans and high rollers from the boardwalk casinos. Eric Clapton dropped by to turn up the blues heat on *Little Red Rooster* (as he had on other stops on the tour), W. Axl Rose and Izzy Stradlin of Guns 'N' Roses did their "junior glimmer twins" thing on a one-night-only performance of *Salt Of The Earth* and the Stones themselves paid tribute to their deep blues roots, bringing on John Lee Hooker to lead them through some feelgood boogie.

The Steel Wheels extravaganza was never about simply making rock history come alive. The Stones rammed that point home every night during *It's Only Rock And Roll*, leaning into the song like they'd just written it the day before, while a pantheon of rock immortals paraded across the video screens - Berry, Holly, Presley, Hendrix, Led Zeppelin and, of course, the spotty '64 Stones. Now, as then, the Stones were out to prove that this was history in the making - and they were far from finished.

HARLEM SHUFFLE

Number six in the evening's hit parade, sandwiched between *Undercover of the Night* and *Tumbling Dice*, the Stones' saucy reading of *Harlem Shuffle* was their loving nod to the gritty urban R&B of the early sixties which they had tried so hard to emulate in their formative years. First waxed by Bob and Earl in 1963, the original *Harlem Shuffle* was a robust dancefloor strut stoked with muscle. On stage - as they did in the studio when they cut the song for *Dirty Work* - the Stones revamped the song into a wonderfully sinuous,

boldly sexual romp, jacking up the guitar aggro while Charlie Watts nailed down the beat with blithe precision. Jagger worked the stage with a cocky flair that would have gone down a storm on audition night at the Apollo Theatre, making the most of the song's down-home lyric flourishes ("Do the monkey, chi-*yi-yi-yi*-ild!"). And when he hit that big opening "Wooo!" at New York's Shea Stadium with backup singers Bernard Fowler, Lisa Fischer and Cindy Mizelle, you can bet they heard it all the way over on 125th.

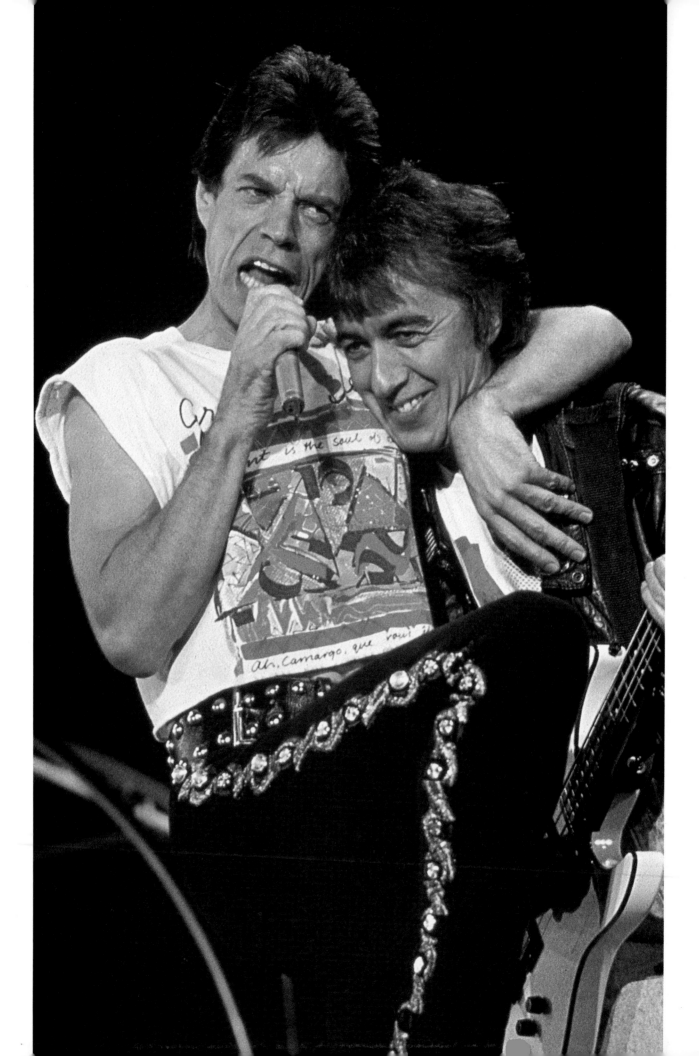

THE STAGE

The beginnings of an abstract thought, an elusive and ephemeral concept, can be a tricky customer to deal with. When Mick Jagger started to think about how the '89-'90 Stones tour would look, he knew that he was going to need help pinning down his ideas. What he wanted was the largest, most elaborate stage set ever constructed for a rock show - and this Herculean task eventually fell to Fisher Park Ltd.

The Stones knew Fisher Park's work from stages they had designed for other major shows, including Tina Turner, Janet Jackson and Pink Floyd's The Wall. Steel Wheels, however, had to be different. Architect Mark Fisher started to turn Jagger's ideas into a visual reality. Sketches and drawings were produced and amended; scale models were constructed and altered. Consulting constantly with Jagger and Charlie Watts, they gradually evolved the design concept, bringing in the lighting and sound designers, too, as Mark and his partner Jonathan Park began to get down to the nuts and bolts of the construction. Of course, it didn't take long to realise that Steel Wheels was too big to be lugged around Europe and, rather than simply scale down the original stage set, a whole new design was needed, retaining all the paradoxical imagery of urban vitality and industrial decay. Fisher presented the first Urban Jungle ideas to the Stones in New York in January 1990 and on Valentine's Day in Tokyo, Mark, Mick and Charlie pored over the final scale model of the show that was poised to take Europe by storm.

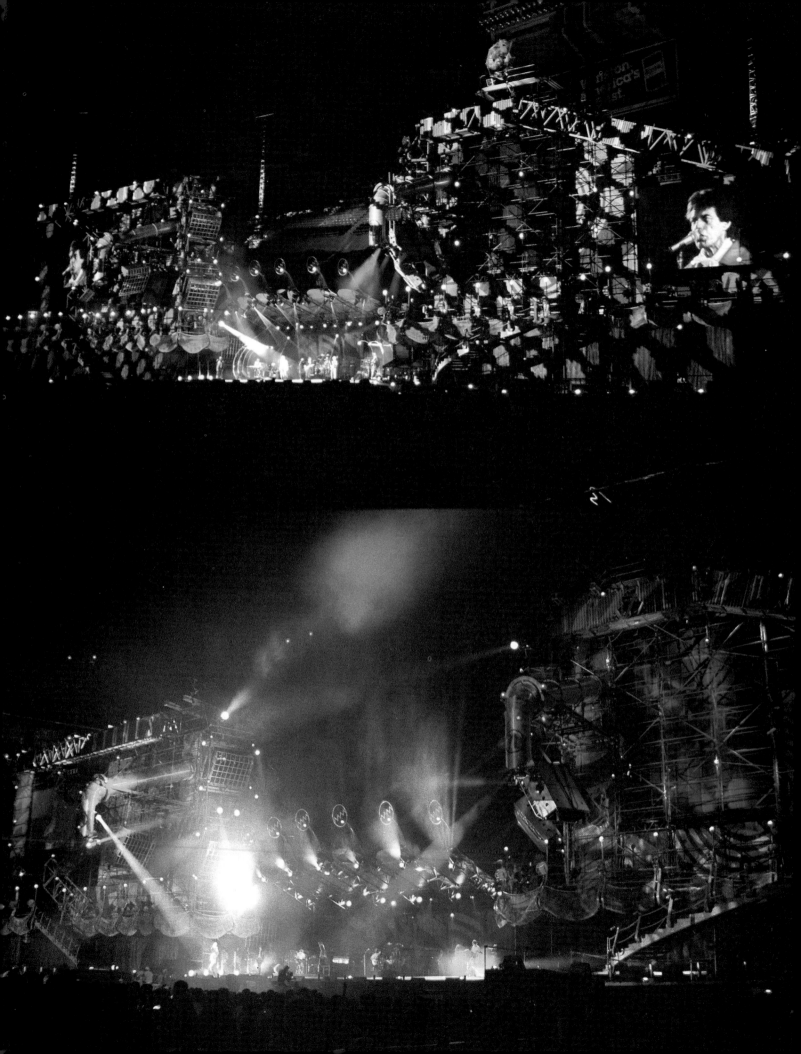

LIGHTS

There had been talk of a Rolling Stones tour. Patrick Woodroffe had worked with Mick Jagger on Jagger's solo tour and there had been talk of how the lighting might be handled should the Stones ever tour again.

A phone call from Barbados brought the flights of fancy into focus. Jagger and Richards were there, working together, planning a new album, planning a tour. It was to be the most spectacular rock show ever staged and it had to have the most spectacular illumination imaginable. Woodroffe was the man with the expertise and inspiration to bring it all together.

The lighting design evolved through a series of meetings, notably in Montserrat where the Stones gathered to begin recording, during which the concepts of the Steel Wheels and Urban Jungle stage designs were formulated.

Woodroffe's idea was to reflect the scale of the stage set, the scale of the venues the band would play and the scale of the events themselves with lighting on an equally fantastic scale. Rather than sprinkle the stage with thousands of smaller lights, Woodroffe settled for just eight colossal 50,000 watt units inspired by the stadium lights. Incorporated in each was a giant Megamac colour scrolling device developed for the tour by Light and Sound Design of Birmingham.

Gels leaked across the front of the lights facilitating an effective and speedy colour change. These massive lights bathed the stage in a selection of twelve colours and were complemented by 70 Varilites and 200 architectural bulkhead lights which helped create the set's image of industrial decay.

In fact, there was as much emphasis placed on lighting the set as there was on lighting the performance area. The entire spectacle was intended to have as much visual appeal from the far end of the stadium as it did from in front of the stage. Those at the back of the crowd had to

be able to respond to the mood of each number even if, from where they were standing, the performance area seemed little bigger than a postage stamp. The same philosophy was employed on both Steel Wheels and Urban Jungle, although the techniques differed.

The Steel Wheels set was dead in daylight. Part of its appeal lay in the way that the dormant structure started to light up and glow as soon as the house lights went down. The whole thing came to life when the Stones hit the stage.

Urban Jungle, on the other hand, had to work visually unaided in the early evening daylight of the European venues, hence the garishly bright colours on the enormous hanging scrims. Rather than having colour slowly becoming apparent in the lighting, the dynamism of the band carried the show until darkness descended and the lighting effects kicked in, adding a whole new dimension to the performance.

Once the philosophizing and the conceptualizing had been turned into tangible lighting hardware, lighting directors Dave Hill and Charlie Wilson took over to run the lighting boards during the shows. Stored on computer were "scenes" Woodroffe, his staff and the band had created together. The lighting boards were then "played" almost like musical instruments to recall the required effects at precisely the right moment. At the same time, the 35 follow spot operators (union hands in the US but truck drivers and roadies in Europe to avoid language difficulties) and pyro technicians positioned all over the rigging followed instructions relayed through headphones.

Although the lighting effects never changed fundamentally from show to show, there was always something new to be incorporated as the whole performance was fine-tuned, adding a more extravagant effect to highlight a guitar solo or pull together a chorus. If it was ever felt that something could be done better, suggestions from all quarters were taken on board.

The most spectacular rock show ever staged, after all, had to have the most spectacular illumination imaginable.

JAPAN

The dark glasses did little to disguise the figure in the blue jacket striding purposefully towards the VIP reception suite. A legend can't hide behind a set of shades.

By his side, shrouded against the February chill in a camel coat and a white scarf was his long-time friend and musical partner. Together they advanced on the massed ranks of photographers and the waiting army of fans.

Mick Jagger and Charlie Watts had arrived at Tokyo's Narita Airport.

The day before, Keith Richards and Ronnie Wood had experienced a similar reception. The Rolling Stones were assembling for their first ever tour of Japan.

Bill Wyman had been delayed and would follow on a few days later, missing out on the Steel Wheels press conference at the Tokyo Dome, the venue for all ten of the Stones' Japanese shows.

The four Rolling Stones who did appear on the low stage for the benefit of the Japanese journalists looked relaxed and rested, having enjoyed a six week break after their exhausting 36 city North American tour. Flanked by an imposing honour guard of Samurai warriors, they smiled good naturedly and fielded a barrage of questions fired at them from the floor. The build-up to the Rolling Stones' Japanese debut had begun.

The days before the first show saw Rolling Stones fever sweep through the city. Massive merchandise displays in Tokyo record stores only served to feed the fans' hunger for anything bearing the band's imprimatur. It was a degree of enthusiasm which, according to the store managers, had never before been seen - not even when Michael Jackson was in town.

The Stones themselves determined to enjoy their stay in Japan. They indulged in a spot of sightseeing and a fun fair at the stadium was closed for the afternoon while the band, their families and some of the tour staff sampled a few thrills and spills. Keith and Ronnie joined the audience at the Tokyo Dome (the shape of the roof earned the venue its nickname, The Big Egg) for Mike Tyson's World Title fight on February 11th, watching usurper Buster Douglas strip the champ of his title.

Tyson, however, wasn't the only one with a headache when the fight finished. As soon as it was all over, the stage crews moved in, ripping out the boxing ring to make way for the Steel Wheels stage. The Japanese riggers had little more than two days before the first show. Everything was waiting, primed and ready to be loaded in, but the stage had never been built in such a short time before.

The show went ahead on schedule, of course, but behind the scenes as the Stones exploded onto the stage, was sprawled a team of weary riggers. Having worked round the clock to complete the erection, many of them simply fell fast asleep, missing the very first Rolling Stones performance in Japan.

Audience reaction to the world's greatest rock and roll band generally varied from a wild enthusiasm to an ecstatic frenzy, but the Japanese audience was something entirely different. Mick had already experienced the phenomenon on his solo tour, but for the rest of the band it was a new sensation. Having come straight from their offices, many of those in the crowd wore sober business suits and carried briefcases. A wave of applause would accompany an appreciated guitar solo or instrumental break and a thunderous roar would follow each number . . . dying to

absolute silence for the start of the next.

Crowd control on leaving the stadium was also markedly different from the anarchic rush and crush at western shows. Each section of the audience waited for an announcement over the PA instructing them to leave, then filed out of the appropriate exits in an orderly fashion - possibly the world's most polite rock 'n' roll rebels.

The band was whisked out of the stadium even before the crowd began its regimented departure. Before The Big Egg was entireley empty they were back in the Hotel Okura in the heart of Tokyo.

Mid-way through the band's stint at The Big Egg, their record company threw a party for a particular celebration. Traditionally, the Japanese celebrate a major occasion, such as a wedding or moving into a new house, with a special sake ceremony. The lid of a wooden cask of the finest sake is smashed open with a wooden mallet and the contents sampled in traditional square wooden cups. The band was presented with a sake cask wrapped in a hemp jacket bearing the legend "The Very Honourable Rolling Stones", which they duly broke open after being awarded a platinum disc for sales of the Steel Wheels CD.

By the time the last fans were trooping out of The Big Egg, over half a million people had seen the Rolling Stones play live in Tokyo and the band's long overdue Japanese inauguration had been declared a resounding success. The day after the last show on February 27th, the Stones and their families went their separate ways, flying home to prepare for a different show on a different continent.

URBAN JUNGLE

The show which finally arrived in Europe in May 1990 and spent the rest of the summer there was a significantly different affair from the mighty Steel Wheels which had trundled across America and Japan. In the first place, the stage set had been completely re-designed. Gone were all those images redolent of dark satanic mills – the chutes, the overhangs, the extruded metallic thingies and chainmail balustrades. The general air of post-industrial mayhem of Steel Wheels had all been replaced by a brighter, lighter and more summery looking structure which relied on swirls of colour rather than tons of armour.

The concept, however, was essentially the same. Steel Wheels had grown out of Jagger's desire to create an industrial urban landscape that "looked more like a forest". This time it was the forest that was starting to look more citified. Both designs took their cue from the slightly futuristic architectural junkheaps portrayed in films such as *Blade Runner* or *Brazil*. Urban Jungle was styled more on the model of a derelict plantation house, overrun by weird mutated foliage and other, even more obstreperous, new life forms.

It sounded like a great idea. Its more compact size solved many of the problems inevitably associated with touring the slow roads of the frontier and customs-clogged territories of Europe. Including site preparation, Urban Jungle could be staged in six days where Steel Wheels needed ten. It weighed less and moved faster. By virtue of being more intrinsically colourful, it was also better suited to the sorts of curfew restrictions which bedevil outdoor rock events in many European cities. Steel Wheels was designed to be seen fully lit and in total darkness: Urban Jungle – like the set the Stones built for their daytime shows in 1982 – would make better sense in the long twilight of a summer evening. And from the band's point of view it offered a refreshing change, a different playing environment from the one they had already strutted and scampered all over on 70 separate occasions.

Despite all its advantages, Urban Jungle proved difficult to get right. The jungly, beast-ridden paintings of an American artist, John Alexander (popular with Jagger and the rest of the Stones), provided a promising starting point. The colourful exotic plants were thought to be fine but all those mandrills, alligators and parrots didn't promote quite the right image. To give the set the raw edge which was required, the tour logo was created. A wild four legged thing with a headful of jagged teeth, the general feeling was that this creature might once have been a dog and it was duly christened Skippy. The deranged canine theme caught on. To compensate for the loss of so many of the 3D elements in the Steel Wheels set, it was suggested that a pack of giant inflatable "Street Fighting Dogs" be introduced to spring into life during the opening bars of *Street Fighting Man*.

The problems came late, almost too late – after the set had been agreed and painted, and only three days before the first show in Rotterdam.

That mutant psychedelic foliage which always looked so good on paper (it was heavily featured in a fold-out centrespread in the official tour programme, and indeed stayed there) simply didn't work when transferred onto fabric scrim. A new design based loosely on images of primitive cave-painting used in the video for the band's single, *Terrifying*, was hurriedly commissioned instead. It didn't look particularly plant-like, but nobody minded – or even seemed to notice – because it looked good anyway. The colour scheme was adjusted as the tour went along.

Meanwhile, all the other specials on the Urban Jungle menu were cooking nicely. Despite the fact that both Steel Wheels and Urban Jungle boasted generous helpings of Stones' classics, neither show was merely a greatest hits package. The concerts were seriously roadtesting songs from *Steel Wheels*, the band's first album in three years. *Mixed Emotions, Sad Sad Sad,* and *Rock And A Hard Place* were in there most nights. *Blinded By Love, Almost Hear You Sigh* and *Terrifying* received regular airings. Keith usually sang *Can't Be Seen* alongside *Happy* in his vocal slot. Of the older tunes, Urban Jungle highlighted one notable absentee from the Steel Wheels set: the anthem for the inflatable doggies, *Street Fighting Man,* had been carefully dusted down and renovated to the same impeccably high standard as everything else.

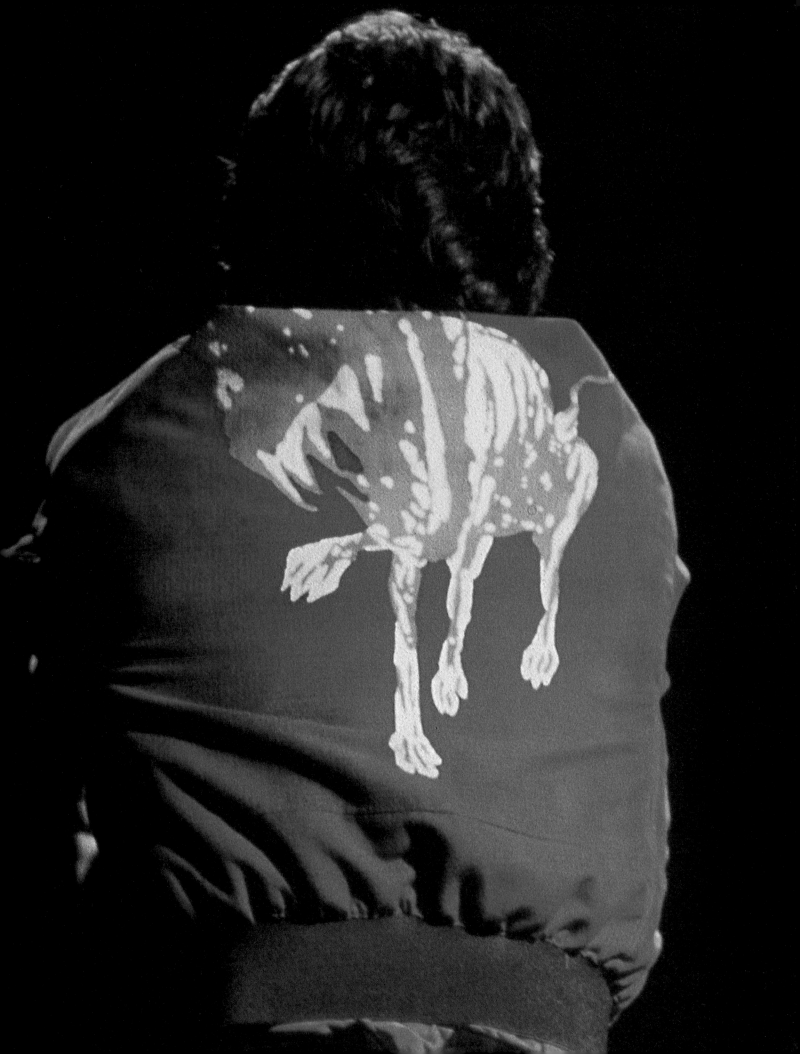

It was this fierce concentration on keeping the music sounding sharp and fresh which really saved the Urban Jungle show from turning into a modified, not to say scaled down, version of Steel Wheels. It would have been easy – and quite understandable – for the Stones to have done what nearly all stadium rock bands now do on The World Tour – drift onto automatic pilot, perform the same songs in the same order every night, line up plenty of backing tapes to airbrush away any sloppiness in the playing . . . and sleepwalk it.

They actually succumbed to none of those options. For the month of April before the European leg, the Stones were back in rehearsal at a chateau in Dangu, near Paris. There were the two new backing singers to drill, some new songs to straighten out and some old ones to reclaim. Whereas in the past the Stones might have left everything to intuition and that old live magic, for this tour they got down to work, painstakingly recreating all of the original arrangements rather than simply busking through an approximation of them. They would regularly

work all through the night to get a song absolutely right. Such was the case with *Street Fighting Man* which they played, straight through, no less than 18 times.

Jagger's view of the Stones' newfound commitment was characteristically sardonic. "There used to be tremendous ups and downs. We'd give a great show then a really sub-standard performance. People were being late for shows, not wanting to do sound checks. I think they thought being lackadaisical was kind of hip. But the tenor of the moment has changed. Now everybody seems really focussed and proud of what they're doing. It's more hip to be professional now."

Maybe it is. Certainly, the sheer professionalism of this show impressed some pretty unlikely people. One Major General Corbett of the Irish Guards paid a surprise visit to Patrick Woodroffe's lighting tower when the Urban Jungle tour played Berlin. The experience of witnessing Woodroffe passing instructions to his 35 pyro and lighting technicians left the good Major General in a bit of a daze.

Sound checks – Keith gives it a thrash,   Ron gives it a scratch and Mick pauses for thought.

It was, he declared afterwards, so well organized it was "just like directing artillery fire."

The ultimate test of the Urban Jungle tour, though, was always going to be its popularity with European audiences. In the States, the Stones commanded unswerving loyalty. Closer to home, and with a recession on the way, nobody could be sure. It had been a long time, etc, etc. In the event, several European stadium shows by big international superstars actually had to be called off or re-scheduled inside smaller, indoor arenas during the summer of 1989; but not the Stones'. The "word of mouth" on this show was uniformly good. Dates were added in nearly every country to which it travelled.

In their own back yard, fickle Britain, the band played to more than twice the number of fans who had turned out in 1982 – a remarkable tribute to what can only be described as the survival of the fittest. Something to do with the law of the (urban) jungle, perhaps.

HONKY TONK WOMEN

The biggest stars of the show every night were, inevitably, the Honky Tonk Women, Angie and Ruby. 60 feet high when fully erect, they were made from four hundredweight of ripstop nylon and needed a tremendous amount of puff (180 cubic metres each, from two huge industrial air conditioning fans) to stay inflated. The problem, once they were up, was to stop them from floating away, as Pink Floyd's pig had done in 1976. A team of between 8 and 12 roadies – depending on the strength of the prevailing wind – was always in place behind the scenes, with guy lines, to make sure that the girls behaved themselves properly. And, despite snagging their stockings a few times on the way up and down, behave they did, to enormous applause. It's hard to see how the Stones will ever be able to perform this song again without them.

INFLATABLES

When the opening bars of *Honky Tonk Women* filled the stadium, Keith Payne's eyes were on the crowd. Those in the crowd, however, only had eyes for Ruby and Angie, the two 60 foot high hookers appearing as if by magic at each side of the stage. The girls were Keith's darlings and watching the audience react to them was always the high point of any show for him.

Ruby and Angie, as well as the rabid dogs which sprang up

stage was required. When it was time to say goodnight to the girls, the fans were thrown into reverse, sucking the air out to collapse the figures. They could then be packed into boxes little bigger than tea chests and the boxes (weighing four or five hundredweight depending on whether the ladies had got wet or not) were loaded onto the trucks for the journey to the next venue.

The dogs, Top Dog, Kennel Dog, Skippy and Shagger

to accompany the band on *Street Fighting Man*, were made by Air Artists of Suffolk, a company which has been creating inflatables for all kinds of stage shows for around 15 years. The inflatables were made from sections of ripstop nylon which were stitched together, then inflated and sprayed by Keith and the crew from his company, Air Brush, hanging from cherry picker crane platforms in the British Airship Industries hangar in Bedford.

On stage the biggest inflatables, the girls, took 30 seconds to inflate with an industrial air conditioning fan breathing life into them at a rate of six cubic metres per second. The air, of course, bled out through the stitching, so the fans continued to blast air into the figures for as long as their presence on

(Shagger contrived to eat Jagger during the show) were also Keith's responsibility. Despite the fact that there were guide cables to help ensure a trouble free inflation and the fact that an inflatable could have up to six roadies keeping it under control in a windy stadium, the dogs and the girls would occasionally foul the rigging and require running repairs and paint touch-ups.

Having taken less than a week to manufacture once the design process was completed, these simple, but highly effective stage props were, according to Keith, relatively easy to look after.

Once every show, Jagger just had to remember to feed Shagger.

To help the band relax on the Steel Wheels tour, pool tables were installed in the tented enclosures backstage. For Urban Jungle in the UK, these were replaced by more "British" snooker tables.

As well as pool or snooker tables, video games were available. To escape from the stress of being Mick Jagger, the Stones' front man would occasionally see how he coped with the pressure of being Nigel Mansel. How Nigel Mansel might feel about fronting the Stones is another matter.

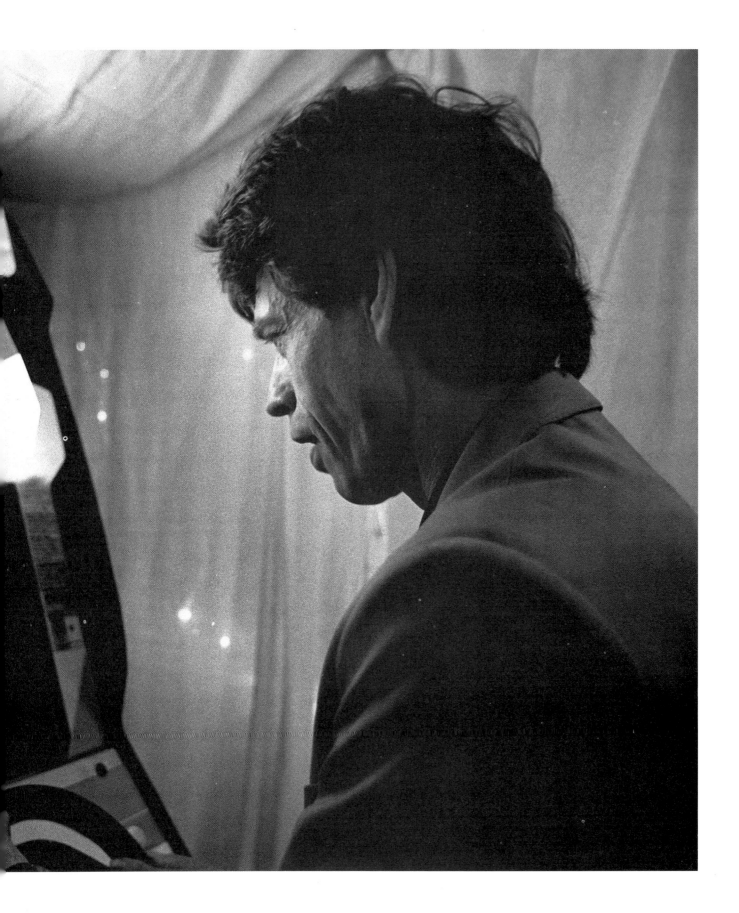

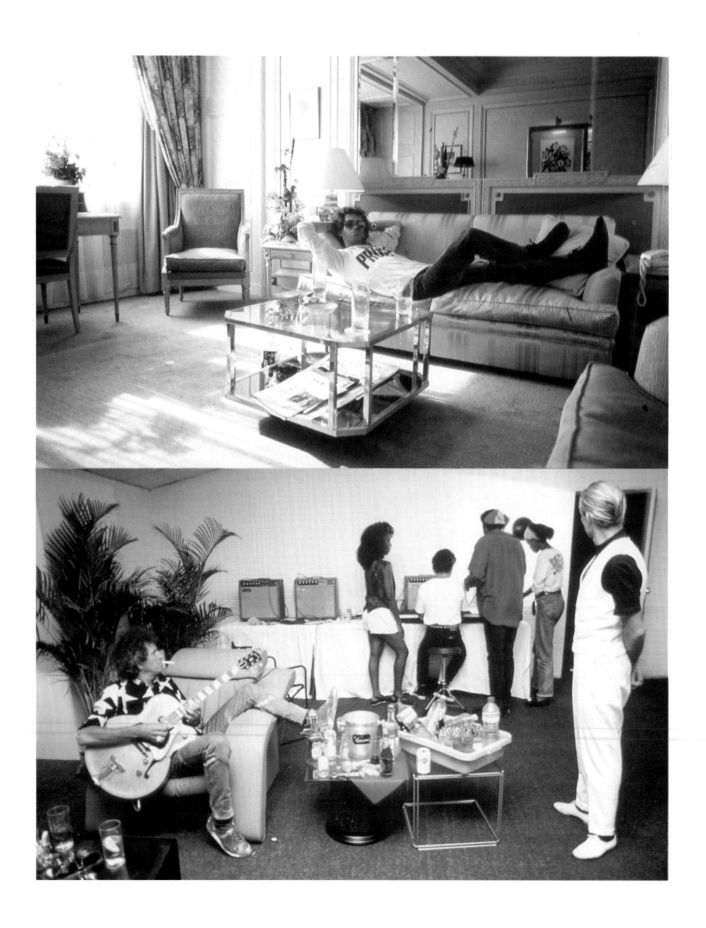

MUSICIANS/BACKING SINGERS

There had never been so many "walk on" parts in a Stones' show as there were for this one. In the end, a carefully selected squad of 10 ancillary players, blowers and singers were needed to get the songs sounding the way the band wanted them – which was, in all cases, exactly the way they had been arranged and recorded in the first place. With no short cuts, and no backing tapes allowed, there was nearly always plenty of extra work to be done.

The most visible and attractive guests at the onstage party were the trio of black backing vocalists down at the front on the left. From Los Angeles to Poplar in East London via Queens, New York they came, trailing some interesting previous work experience. Bernard Fowler, from NYC, had taken time out from his day job with Tackhead, the uncompromisingly hard rock/dance outfit, to let his sweet tenor voice be heard more clearly on songs like *Ruby Tuesday*. Lorelei McBroom, from LA, was a singer/songwriter in her own right with a long list of "also sang" credits for artists such as Pink Floyd, Lou Reed and Billy Idol. Sophia Jones, from London, E14, had helped out U2 on their Rattle and Hum tour.

Sophia and Lorelei joined Bernard for the Urban Jungle tour, but for Steel Wheels he had enjoyed the company of two different young ladies. Lisa Fischer from Brooklyn had recorded with artists like Billy Ocean and Dione Warwick and toured with Chaka Khan and a certain Mr Michael Philip Jagger. Cindy Mizelle, from Englewood New Jersey, had - like Lisa - a host of impressive credits to her name. As well as writing and performing her own songs, she had accompanied Carly Simon, Melba Moore, Freddie Jackson and Chaka Khan to name but a few.

The horns looked rather more used and sounded a lot more familiar. The baritone sax man Bobby Keys had been playing regularly with the Stones for 20 years. Along with Jim Price, he had been their brass section, period, on most of the classic albums of the 70s. In 1988 he was signed up by Keith Richards for his solo project, the X-pensive Winos. For this tour Keys was joined by the four piece Uptown Horns, a curious looking quartet of no fixed haircut who could nevertheless deliver a fiercely brassy punch and who numbered James Brown and Tom Waits among their regular clients.

Over the course of the two and a half hour show, horn players and backing singers came and went, retiring to their respective cubby holes somewhere up inside the

Previous pages
(left) Sophia Jones, Bernard Fowler and
Lorelei McBroom lend the Stones some vocal
support.
(right) The Uptown Horns provide a blast of
brass and plenty of style.

(above) Matt Clifford gives Bill a better view.
(centre) Chuck Leavell
(right) Matt Clifford

vast Urban Jungle edifice when they weren't needed. The
Stones' two keyboard operatives, however, never left
their posts. Chuck Leavell, a veteran of the 1982 tour and
sometime Allman Brother, took care of the straight,
rhythmic piano parts: boogie woogying (*Honky Tonk
Women*) or rocking out (*Sympathy for the Devil*) as the
occasion demanded.

Young Matt Clifford, on the other hand, had a rather
different brief. Having been rescued by Mick Jagger from
the jaws of Anderson, Bruford, Wakeman and Howe – it

was his job to rummage through a bank of computerised keyboard and sampling equipment to find the orchestral voices needed for songs like *As Tears Go By, Ruby Tuesday* and *2000 Light Years From Home*. He also played the French horn at the beginning of *You Can't Always Get What You Want.*

The textural sophistication of the show relied heavily on the talents of the backing singers and musicians and the applause which was so warmly afforded them was richly deserved.

MIDNIGHT RAMBLER

Nothing in the whole performance demonstrated the band's confidence in their own musicianship better than this long and brilliantly paced account of the old rude blues favourite, *Midnight Rambler*. Jagger is usually judged on his dancing, his prancing, his dress sense and – sometimes – his singing. Here he served a belting reminder that he can still play the blues harmonica as well as anyone, and has now, thanks to his solo tour perhaps, become a pretty proficient rhythm guitarist into the bargain. The real beauty of this song lay in its quieter parts. In a sense, anybody can put together a big stadium show but few have the necessary charisma – or nerve – to leave the tricks aside and hold a vast crowd in thrall to just a voice and a guitar. There may have been more exciting moments in the show, but there were none more bold and magical.

To get from one venue to another on time, it was essential that the Stones had an aircraft on hand. In the States a Boeing 707 was at their disposal. For the band's various hops around Europe, aircraft charter brokers Chapman Freeborn laid on a selection of planes ranging from a 78 seat DC-9 to a 168 seat MD-3.

The Urban Jungle tour logo was the inspiration for the four rabid dogs which erupted onto the stage during *Street Fighting Man*. Everyone was determined that Urban Jungle should not give the impression of being simply a poor relation to Steel Wheels. The European show had to be a unique experience.

HAPPY

Everybody was playing better on this tour than they had perhaps ever played before, none more so than in the guitars department. Keith Richards' commitment to living rock and roll is surpassed only by his enormous enthusiasm for playing it. The frequent flash of that familiar grin was seen so often on the tour that there could be no doubt as to how much Keith was enjoying being back on stage with the Rolling Stones.

No one could have been more disappointed than Keith Richards, then, when two shows at London's Wembley Stadium had to be postponed when a septic finger put him out of action. Postponing the shows was an agonising decision, but an inevitable one. Offering a packed stadium in the Stones' "own back yard" a substandard performance was unthinkable, especially given how consistently well Richards had been playing.

Perhaps, like Jagger, Keith's stunning performances stemmed from the discipline imposed by his solo album and tour in 1988; maybe he was just on a roll. Either way, there was no mistaking the cocksure class of his playing this time. From the slashing opening of *Start Me Up* through to the steaming finale, *Satisfaction*, Keith was on the case, particularly so during the two song segment when Jagger left the stage to him. *Happy*, his vocal debut from *Exile On Main Street* was an obvious choice and crowd pleaser for Richards' solo spot.

Either *Before They Make Me Run (Some Girls)* or *Cant Be Seen* from *Steel Wheels*, provided the second number of the interlude before the Richards generator was back on line as the powerhouse behind the main performance.

FANS

It had been almost eight years since the band had last played live together and all the months of planning, preparation and rehearsal which went in before Steel Wheels took to the road proved that the Rolling Stones were determined not to disappoint their fans.

The fans, on the other hand, were just as determined not to disappoint the band. The capacity crowds in stadia on three continents included legions of stalwart Stones supporters from the sixties as well as younger fans, many of whom had barely been cutting their first teeth when the Stones were cutting their first record. Many, indeed, hadn't even been born in the sixties.

Bridging any real or imagined generation gap, the Stones

played to over six million devotees worldwide. Maybe some had dusted off a memory or two in recalling the lyrics of *Ruby Tuesday* or *Let's Spend The Night Together*, maybe some had the songs fresh in their minds, but none could have put more effort into singing along than the fans in Japan.

Learning songs verbatim from a recording sung in a peculiar dialect of a particularly difficult foreign language is a daunting undertaking, but the Tokyo Dome stood witness to thousands of fans chanting lines like:

I met a gin soaked bar room queen in Memphis
and
I was raised by a toothless bearded hag!

The Stones weren't performing alone at any show. They had the best support they could ever have hoped for . . . their own audience

Production Coordinator Michael Ahern (centre) talking to Mick Jagger and sound man Benji Lefevre.

SOUND

Steel Wheels and Urban Jungle were designed for maximum visual impact but the months of painstaking creative planning spent blending the stage concepts with the lighting design and the Stones' set list would have amounted to sheer folly if particular attention had not been paid to the sound system.

The man brought in to mastermind the audio arrangements was Benji Lefevre. With almost 25 years' experience of touring with rock bands, Benji had a shrewd idea of the sort of problems the band would face in taking such a massive stage show all around the world.

Lefevre looked to Showco, of Dallas, Texas, to supply the equipment he needed and with the two complete Steel Wheels sound systems on the road in the U.S., he needed plenty. Much of the hardware had to be specially manufactured for the tour.

Each show required 80 tons of sound gear transported in six 44 foot articulated trucks. A whole truck was required for the amps and sub bass speaker enclosures. Another carried the stage left speakers, another the stage right speakers and yet another took care of the stage monitors.

Lefevre's field delay system filled a truck all on its own. The digitally delayed speakers were mounted on carefully designed towers during a show, arranged with mathematical precision around the stadium to ensure an even and efficient spread of sound throughout the arena without obstructing the view of the stage for any of the audience.

The stacks on the stage itself reached up to a giddy 65 ft, again to ensure that those furthest from the stage could hear everything every bit as well as those right at the front. The stage was designed with a floored roadway below it specifically for moving the sound gear into position as quickly and smoothly as possible.

Two complete 10 man sound crews worked on the Steel Wheels stages in the U.S. as well as a universal team of six

who travelled from show to show. For Urban Jungle, a 12 strong team travelled from one venue to another. Each crew member spent two days at the rehearsal stage in Nassau learning exactly how the equipment should be installed and each was provided with a personal copy of the sound system design and wiring layout. Each of the crew had a specific job to do and it was imperative that they knew exactly where every element of the sound system should be for everything to be loaded in and out of the stadia efficiently.

To this end, the sound crews also had to work in harmony with the riggers and lighting crews. Cooperation was the key work in loading in and out of a stadium quickly. During the show Lefevre controlled the sound from his mixing desk, fine tuning the system at the same time to compensate for imponderables such as vagaries in the weather, whilst his crew monitored the equipment, poised, for example, to replace an amplifier on the spot should it begin to show problematic symptoms.

Wear and tear on the equipment was dealt with on the road. A technician travelled with the tour diagnosing faults and effecting repairs and maintenance on the electronics. Lefevre took a "hands on" role here, too, even turning his hand to a spot of carpentry when speaker cabinets, swollen by the rain, refused to fit into their alloted truck space. Essential spares were available to cater for maintenance which might put any element of the sound system out of action. Around 150 substitute speakers of different sizes were carried on the tour. Sending to Dallas for a replacement should something malfunction was out of the question.

Venues were also viewed with a critical eye when it came to maintaining sound quality. In Pittsburgh a 160 foot long glass fronted press enclosure was found to be reflecting sound to an unacceptable degree. The whole enclosure was simply masked off with specially made black drapes.

Throughout the whole tour the band, and especially Mick and Keith, were heavily involved with the sound crews, giving and taking advice and criticism with just one thought in mind; to stage the best possible Rolling Stones performance, and at the next gig, to make it even better.

2000 LIGHT YEARS FROM HOME

While nobody could accuse the Stones of being an art-rock band, the show did contain some bits which might have confused Chuck Berry, and *2000 Light Years From Home* was definitely one of them. Recorded in 1967 for the *Satanic Majesties* album, it had never been performed live before because of the problems involved in recreating that delicate swirl of sound which surrounds Jagger's psychedelic vocal. Now Matt Clifford's machines had sorted all that out, leaving the stage free for Mick Jagger to essay a spot of modern dance beneath one of Patrick Woodroffe's most strikingly atmospheric lighting designs. The choreography, like everything else, had not been left to chance or the inspiration of the moment. Jagger was coached for this languid, snakey routine by the British modern dance choreographer, Ben Craft and his American counterpart Lavelle Smith.

SYMPATHY FOR THE DEVIL

It's sometimes referred to as the "Cor! Fuck!" factor, and every Stones spectacular has to have one in it somewhere. It's the main *coup de theatre* of the evening, or, if you prefer, a colossally extravagant item of visual gimmickry. On the 1982 tour, it involved Jagger being plucked out of the PA stacks at the side of the stage by a cherry picker and whirled over the heads of the audience. For this outing, he was secretly whisked up to the top of the set in a special elevator to perform *Sympathy For The Devil* about a hundred feet or so above the rest of the band. A slightly risky stunt, which must have added considerably to the tour's insurance bill, it passed almost completely without mishap except at Hannover in Germany when Jagger's mike wouldn't work, forcing him back down again, sharpish.

IT'S ONLY ROCK AND ROLL

It may be a clichéd turn of phrase but this, maybe more than any other Stones hit certainly deserves its status as a "classic rock anthem". The timeless energy and raw edge of *It's Only Rock and Roll* belie the fact that the song is more than 16 years old.

Performing it on stage for this tour, the Stones had the best backing any rock band could imagine. To accompany the classic song, classic film footage filled the huge video screens at either side of the stage and the Stones cavorted alongside a host of rock heroes from Buddy Holly and Chuck Berry to David Bowie and Led Zeppelin.

Also up there on screen were the wan images of the '60s vintage Rolling Stones.

LOGISTICS

Moving Steel Wheels around America, Japan and Europe was like taking an army to war or, more accurately, like grafting an industrial complex onto a selected city then swiftly transplanting it to another.

Venues for the shows were vetted months in advance, not only for capacity, location or availability, but also to establish whether the city in question could actually cope with staging the show. Local labour requirements and the impact on the local infrastructure would be considerable.

Six days before the Urban Jungle show (ten for Steel Wheels) the advance guard would arrive to begin site preparation, putting up tents, installing offices, phone lines, catering and medical facilities and making sure that the locally hired machinery - fork lifts, scissor lifts, cranes, etc. - was in position.

The next day, 75 scaffolders would show up, just ahead of 11 truckloads of scaffolding (known as "steel"). Each truck could have two drivers, so already almost 100 newcomers would be looking for food, coffee, showers, soap, towels and a phone to call home. Work in the stadium during this period would start at around six in the morning and probably not end until around midnight.

Around noon on the day before the show, what became known as "the buses from hell" would arrive. Up to ten buses would disgorge around 150 tour personnel, most of whom had generally got out of the wrong side of the bed (or bus) and weren't in the best of moods. Although the coaches were well-appointed with beds, toilets, shower and cooking facilities as well as video systems, all the weary travellers really wanted to do *en route* was to get some sleep. When they spilled out of the buses they too were looking for food, coffee, showers, etc., etc.

Local labour in the form of stage hands and security staff could amount to 400, swelling the ever growing population of the Stones' emergent industrial sprawl still further.

By the time the rest of the stage set, the sound and the lighting trucks rolled in, parking space for up to 38 forty four foot articulated units would be taken up. The Scania, Volvo and Daf trucks would arrive at intervals of between half an hour and an hour, having left their previous venue in that order.

Everything was packed into the trucks in a specific order at one show and loaded out at the next destination in the same fashion. Many items were, in fact, dismantled and loaded as soon as their usefulness on stage was at an end as long as this didn't interfere in any way with the performance. The loading process was constantly updated. More hands were added here or a truck pack redefined there to shave vital minutes off the load in and load out times.

When the show was all over and the public were trooping home with *Satisfaction* still ringing in their ears, the mobile industrial complex was

already on the move. The circus which took six days to set up was loaded out in as many hours and "the buses from hell" were on their way to a new destination.

The logistical problems, of course, weren't all centred around just one location. At any one time the show could be touching four different cities with five different 30 ton sets of steel on the road. If the itinerary changed, eleven trucks headed for Italy might suddenly be required in Austria with all the requisite paperwork and official stamps in order for crossing a different border. If there happened to be a hold-up at a border post, a path could sometimes be smoothed through the

stony ground of bureaucracy with a few freebie t-shirts or albums. The truck team leaders had a ready supply specifically for that purpose.

The years of experience accumulated by the personnel involved were what made the whole operation hang together. The dedication and sheer enthusiasm of the tour staff were summed up by Steve Thomas, one of those with the unenviable task of solving problems before they occurred. When asked why he still loved the frantic nomadic lifestyle so much after more than 17 years on tour with rock bands, he replied, "Hell, it's better than selling shoes to fat women!"

GUESTS

The most important guests at any Rolling Stones show are the fans who fill the stadium but there are always plenty of personal friends and familiar faces (all big fans, too, of course!) whom the Stones will want to greet in person.

Pictured on these pages are just some of the celebrity guests privileged enough to have spent some time backstage with the band.

Top row (left to right) – Bruce Springsteen, Patti Sciaffa, Mick; Keith, Steve Winwood,

Bill; Keith, Eric Clapton; Tom Waits, Barbara Orbison.

Middle row (left to right) – W. Axl Rose, Charlie; Rob Lowe, James Belushi; Keith, David Bowie, Ronnie; Charlie, Ringo Starr.

Bottom row (left to right) – Mick with Michael Douglas, Anjelica Houston, Barbara Streisand, Meryl Streep, Jerry Hall; Charlie, Elton John, Mick; Michael Hutchence, Keith; Ringo Starr, Mick.

SATISFACTION

It was never supposed to end, here. The final night of the Urban Jungle tour had been planned to come down somewhere in Eastern Europe; but Keith's infected finger put paid to that. The last two shows of the Stones' run at Wembley Stadium in July had had to be postponed because of the injury, and so it came to pass that the ultimate episodes in this 45 part European adventure unfolded back in England on August 24 and 25.

But the show that played Wembley for the second time wasn't Urban Jungle at all, it was Steel Wheels. As if they hadn't done enough already, the Stones were making a concert film to commemorate the whole expedition, and so had recalled the monstrous metallic fantasy which they'd last seen in Japan in January. Staging Steel Wheels at Wembley was, frankly, a headache. Local authority health and safety restrictions meant there could be no aerial fireworks at the end. And the pitch's natural turf wouldn't stand the greater weight of the set. And the concert had to be over by 10.30 pm. And so on. But it happened. Musically, little things went wrong, as they often can do when the Stones find cameras pointing at them, but the atmosphere on the Saturday night was as highly charged as at any rock concert in recent memory. Everybody knew that this thing which had taken up such an inordinate amount of cultural space for nearly a year was about to disappear for good. And, in a storm of golden fairy dust, it did.

TOUR PERSONNEL

(usa)

Ahern, Michael – Production Coordinator
Aleck, Patricia – Travel Advance
Allison, Mike – Sound Technician
Anderson, Rick – Lighting Technician
Armstrong, Tom – Site Coordinator
Bakal, Jerry – Carpenter
Baptista, Joe – Site Coordinator
Bark, Paul – Varilite Technician
Batty, Bob – Lighting Technician
Beck, Dennis – Staging
Bender, Bob – Security
Benjamin, Guy – Panni Projectionist
Berger, Bill – Carpenter
Bernett, Tim – Travel Advance
Boehning, Wayne – Lighting Technician
Bouman, John – Pyro Technician
Brade, Rowan – Security
Briggs, Randy – Panni Projectionist
Brown, John – Staging
Buess, Pete – Sound Technician
Callaghan, James – Security Chief
Campion, Edmund – Electrician
Campion, John – Master Electrician
Caraffa, Nick – Staging
Carroll, Bob – Rigger
Carter, Clay – Rigger
Carus-Wilson, Simon – Lighting Technician
Caston, Monica – Video Camera Operator
Chavarris, Patricia – Production Assistant
Chavarris, Paul – Production Manager
Clements, Caroline – Makeup
Cofield, Michael – Pyro Technician
Cohl, Michael – Tour Director
Collins, Benny – Site Coordinator
Combs, Gene – Staging
Compton, Collin – Varilite Technician
Condon, Jeff – Merchandising
Conyers, David – Sound Technician
Cooke, Steven – Inflatables
Damas, Stan – Police Liaison
Daniel, Peter – Video Projectionist
Debeauport, Pierre – Guitar Technician

Delahanty, Jim – Rigging Supervisor
Duncan, Gerry – Promoter Production Coordinator
Dunn, Alan – Logistics
Dunn, Arnold – Band Road Manager
Efron, Paul – Carpenter
Eike, Torje – Physiotherapist
Elder, Mike – Promoter Production Assistant
England, Mark – Lighting Technician
Epstein, Gary – Sound Technician
Farese, Michael – Carpenter
Farrugia, Sam – Carpenter
Fisher, Mark – Set Design and Art Direction
Fogel, Arthur – Assistant Tour Promoter
Fortune, Jay – Carpenter
Friedman, Neil – Assistant Tour Publicist
Garabedian, Michael – Carpenter
Garrett, Todd – Sound Technician
Gilleland, Jerry – Tour Production Manager
Gnesin, Fern – Dressing Rooms
Goldman, Donna – Production Office Coordinator
Graham, Kenny – Site Coordinator
Green, Colin – Lighting Technician
Grenier, Bob – Rigging Supervisor
Griffin, Neal – Video Projectionist
Guinness, Miranda – Assistant to Mr. Jagger
Harbin, Eddie – Sound Technician
Hatfield, Tim – Sound Technician
Haynes, Bruce – Electrician
Hendrick, Shane – Electrician
Hill, David – Varilite Director
Hooker, Rusty – Promoter Accountant
Horgan, William – Security
Howard, Jo – Assistant to Mr. Wood
Howard, Steve – Promoter Production Manager
Huffman, Dan – Sound Technician
Hurwitz, Bob – Tour Accountant
Jackson, Helena – Video Camera Operator
Jones, Dennis – Rigger
Jones, Nick – Merchandising
Kim, Uiyung – Pyro Technician
King, Elizabeth – Lighting Technician

King, Tony – Press Liaison
Kittrell, Beth – Administrative Assistant
Kleinberg, Bennett – Advance Tour Publicist
Kohorn, Mark – Carpenter
Lakota, Anne – Video Camera Operator
Lamb, Roy – Stage Manager
Lashells, David – Carpenter
Lazar, Shelley – Ticket/Credentials Coordinator
Lefevre, Benji – House Audio Engineer
Machado, Dan – Sound Technician
Magee, Church – Band Crew Chief
Magnason, Bruce – Staging
Mayne, Rich – Site Coordinator
McGinnis, Jeff – Sound Technician
McGuire, Dennis – Video Engineer
McLeod, Robin – Video Camera Operator
Moncrief, David – Sound Technician
Moncrief, Lon – Staging
Morphy, Dave – Lighting Technician
Newlin, Mark – Sound Technician
Nolan, Steve – Lighting Technician
O'Brien, Kevin – Varilite Technician
Ogilvie-Grant, Alex – Production Assistant
Olean, Steve – Rigger
Oliver, Bea – Carpenter
Panaci, Mic – Lighting Technician
Park, Jonathan – Set Designer
Parker, Steve – Inflatables
Patterson, Matt – Lighting Technician
Payne, Keith – Inflatables
Perry, Norman – Assistant Tour Director
Pickering, Robern – Wardrobe
Putnam, Jim – Sound Technician
Randel, Gary – Varilite Technician
Reaves, Ron – Sound Technician
Richardson, Shawn – Assistant Lighting Director
Richardson, Bob – Carpenter
Richie, Russel – Lighting Technician
Rickards, Joel – Lighting Techinician
Riggio, Jaye – Assistant to the

Rongo, Steve – Carpenter
Rosen, Mike – Carpenter
Russell, Tony – Assistant to Mr. Richards
Safari, Dimo – Photographer
Sakowicz, Joseph – Band/Entourage Luggage
Scovill, Scott – Video Projectionist
Seabrook, Joe – Security
Shepard, Dave – Lighting Technician
Shepherd, Stephen – Drum Technician
Sinclair, David – Electrician
Smith, Greg – Sound Technician
Smith, Lavelle – Choreographer
Stallbaumer, David – Production Manager
Stewart, Dan – Lighting Technician
Strand, Christine – Video Director
Sullivan, Brian – Merchandising
Sutherland, Angus – Guitar Technician
Swink, Ed – Staging
Tanzman, Linn – Press Representative
Thomas, Steve – Promoter Advance Coordinator
Thomson, John – Lead Carpenter
Thonus, Steve – Staging
Topeka, Andy – Keyboard Technician
Torffield, Marvin – On Air Projection
Towne, Andy – Video Projectionist
Townsend, Mary – Staging
Wade, Glen – Panni Projectionist
Wade-Evans, Chris – Monitor Audio Engineer
Ward, Scott – Pyro Technician
Ward, Scott – Rigger
Wein, Bob – Promoter Security Director
Wiesman, Michael – Lead Carpenter
Wetzell, Henry – Electrician
Whitt, Vinnie – Carpenter
Wille, Randy – Sound Technician
Williams, Fiona – Stylist
Wilson, Charlie – Lighting Technician
Woodroffe, Patrick – Lighting Designer and Art Director
Woolley, Timm – Financial Controller
Wright, Joe – Electrican

TOUR PERSONNEL
(europe)

Ahern, Michael – Production Coordinator
Allison, Michael – Audio Technician
Armstrong, Thomas – Site Coordinator
Armstrong, John – Staging Crew Chief
Ashurst, Peter – Staging Crew
Austin, Tracy – Catering
Bailey, Rob – Driver
Bakal, Gerald – Carpenter
Banks, Janet – Catering
Baptista, Joseph – Site Coordinator
Barad, Gerry – Merchandising
Barker, Henry – Driver
Barton, Nicholas – Varilite Technician
Batty, Robert – Lighting Technician
Bedigan, Pete – Driver
Bell, Peter – Pyro Technician
Bender, Bob – Security
Berger, William – Carpenter
Bernett, Timothy – Production Travel
Bollem, Micky – Driver
Brade, Rowan – Security
Brandner, Briggie – Hotel Advance
Bricusse, Paul – Driver
Brockman, Tim – Promoter Security
Bruford, Ian – Staging Crew
Bryce, Neal – Driver
Burke, Peter – Driver
Burns, Lil – Promoter Production Assistant
Calderon, Tracy – Camera Operator
Callaghan, James – Security Chief
Campion, Edmund – Electrician
Campion, John – Chief Electrician
Candles, Andy – Driver
Carter, Clay – Rigger
Caston, Monica – Camera Operator
Cheevers-Hunter, Mandy – Catering
Clarke, Steve – Driver
Claude, Aline – Administrative Assistant
Clements, Paul – Site Coordinator
Clements, Caroline – Makeup
Cody, Matt – Staging Crew
Cody, Tim – Staging Crew
Cohl, Michael – Tour Director
Collins, Les – Driver
Conafray, Mick – Driver
Conk, John – Site Coordinator
Conyers, David – Audio Crew Chief
Cooke, Jan – Driver
Cooke, Ystffan – Inflatables
Craddock, Terrence – Staging Crew
Craft, Ben – Choreographer
Crawford, Anne – Catering
Crust, Alison – Catering
Cubbin, John – Driver
Curtis, Lynn – Assistant to Norman Perry
Daniels, Peter – Video Projectionist
Debeauport, Pierre – Guitar Technician
Devenish, Val – Catering
Dickens, Terry – Staging Crew
Doherty, Bernard – Senior Press Representative
Drury, Gary – Driver

Dunn, Alan – Logistics
Dunn, Arnold – Band Road Manager
Edwards, Eddie – Starvision Technician
Efron, Paul – Advance Carpenter
Eike, Torje – Physiotherapist
Elstar, Elayne – Catering
England, Mark – Lighting Technician
Epstein, Gary – Audio Technician
Evans, Stretch – Staging Crew
Farrugia, Sam – Carpenter
Fellows, Mary – Production Assistant
Fennell, Mitch – Promoter Site Coordinator
Fennic, Bruce – Driver
Figley, Mary Lou – Promoter Site Coordinator
Fish, Suzanne – Catering
Fish, Marlene – Catering
Fisher, Mark – Set Design and Art Direction
Footit, Paul – Driver
Footman, Lorraine – Catering
Fortune, Jay – Carpenter
Fox, David – Driver
Franklin, Mike – Driver
Friedman, Neil – Press Representative
Gilleland, Jerry – Production Manager
Gnesin, Fern – Dressing Rooms
Goldman, Donna – Production Office Coordinator
Grabham, Sandi – Catering
Graham, Kenny – Site Coordinator
Graham, Mick – Driver
Gray, Alan – Pyro Technician
Green, Colin – Lighting Technician
Greenberg, Robbie – Varilite Technician
Grenier, Robert – Rigging Supervisor
Griffin, Neal – Video Projectionist
Guinness, Miranda – Assistant to Mr. Jagger
Hall, Stuart – Starvision Technician
Haltin, Paul – Driver
Hampson, Nicki – Catering
Harbin, Joseph – Audio Technician
Harkness, Desmond – Catering
Harrison, Tim – Driver
Hayward, Paul – Driver
Hill, David – Varilite Director
Hill, Dave – Driver
Hill, Mick – Driver
Hinde, Dave – Staging Crew
Hockabout, Eleanor – Promoter Production Assistant
Holcroft, Terry – Driver
Horgan, William – Security
Howard, Stephen – Promoter Production Manager
Howard, Jo – Assistant to Mr. Wood
Howell, Eric – Driver
Huffman, Daniel – Audio Techncian
Hunter, Ian – Catering
Hurd, John – Staging Crew
Hurlocker, Anthony – Electrician
James, Simon – Staging Crew
Jobson, Graham – Driver
Jones, Alan – Driver
Jones, Nick – Merchandising
Juggins, Graham – Driver

Keating, Tim – Staging Crew
Kennedy, Owen – Catering
Kent, Peter – Catering
Khan, Tariq – Staging Crew
King, Tony – Press Liaison
Kite, Ollie – Trucking Coordinator
Klvana, Cynthia – Production Assistant
Kohorn, Mark – Carpenter
Lakota, Anne – Camera Operator
Lawrence, Albert – Promoter Site Coordinator
Lazar, Shelley – Tickets/Credentials Coordinator
Leary, Steve – Staging Crew
Lefevre, Benji – Audio Engineer
Leonard, Emma – Catering
Lewis, Gary – Staging Crew
Lewis, Jon – Driver
Lowes, Linda – Catering
Luxford, Bud – Merchandising
Lythe, Gary – Staging Crew
Magee, Chuch – Band Crew Chief
Maggiore, Ian – Catering
Marsden, Roderick – Merchandising Accountant
Marshall, Baz – Driver
McIves, Ian – Driver
McManus, Robin – Staging Crew
Meereis, Paul – Driver
Moncrieffe, David – Audio Technician
Moole, Alan – Driver
Morgan, Tarquin – Staging Crew Chief
Moynihan, Chris – Driver
Mutton, Colin – Entourage Accountant
Nash, Julian – Driver
Neuegebauer, David – Camera Operator
Newlin, Mark – Audio Technician
Nolan, Daniel – Lighting Technician
Nolan, Stephen – Lighting Crew Chief
O'Brien, Terry – Driver
Ogilvie-Grant, Alex – Assistant Financial Controller
Oliver, Bea – Carpenter
Orsburn, Terry – Assistant to Mr. Wyman
Otremba, Bob – Video Projectionist
Park, Jonathan – Set Design
Parker, Steve – Carpenter
Payne, Keith – Inflatables
Peck, Simon – Staging Crew
Pelly, Danny – Driver
Perry, Norman – Assistant Tour Director
Pescod, Phillip – Staging Crew
Phillips, Timothy – Lighting Technician
Pirt, Chris – Driver
Putnam, Jim – Audio Technician
Radant, Christine – Production Travel Advance
Reis, Gregory – Camera Operator
Riggio, Jaye – Assistant to Michael Cohl
Robbins, Marc – Promoter Tour Accountant
Robinson, Thomas – Production Assistant
Robinson, Marcus – Varilite Technician

Roddy, Frank – Driver
Rongo, Stephen – Carpenter
Rufo, Celeste – Camera Operator
Rulter, Paul – Driver
Russell, Tony – Assistant to Mr. Richards
Richardson, Robert – Carpenter
Sakowicz, Joseph – Logistics Assistant
Saunders, Ollie – Staging Crew
Scovill, Scott – Video Projectionist
Seabrook, Joseph – Security
Sen, Jane – Press Representative
Shea, Paul – Driver
Sheldrake, Fleur – Catering
Shepard, Stephen – Drum Technician
Simcox, Brian – Driver
Simcox, Chris – Driver
Simpson, Phil – Driver
Simpson, Chris – Driver
Sloan, Alan – Advance Press Representative
Spieser, Tom – Staging Crew
Stallbaumer, David – Stage Manager
Stebulitis, Jed – Driver
Stengel, George – Staging Crew
Stokes, Suzi – Wardrobe
Strand, Christine – Video Director
Stuart, Daniel – Audio Technician
Sullivan, Jim – Merchandising
Sutherland, Angus – Guitar Technician
Sutton, Albert – Driver
Talbot, Denise – Catering
Taylor, Mick – Driver
Thomas, Treys – Promoter Production Accountant
Thomas, Stephen – Promoter Production Advance
Thomas, David – Catering
Thomas, Roger – Driver
Thompson, Chris – Driver
Thompson, Brian – Driver
Topeka, Andy – Keyboard Technician
Townsend, Andy – Staging Crew
Tupper, Carl – Driver
Underwood, Tony – Driver
Vernall, Steve – Driver
Wade-Evans, Christopher – Monitor Engineer
Walker, Greg – Staging Crew
Warnock, Neil – Booking Coordinator
Watts, Bill – Staging Crew
Watts, Ollie – Staging Crew Chief
Wein, Bob – Promoter Security Director
Wetzel, Henry – Electrician
White, David – Starvision Technician
White, Linda – Catering
White, Ray – Starvision Technician
Whitt, Vinnie – Advance Carpenter
Widowson, Derek – Driver
Wiesman, Michael – Assistant Stage Manager
Wille, Randall – Audio Technician
Williams, Fiona – Stylist
Wilson, Charlie – Lighting Board Operator
Wolters, Rande – Rigger
Woodroffe, Patrick – Lighting Designer & Art Direction
Woolley, Timm – Financial Controller
Wynne, Joseph – Staging Crew

TOUR PERSONNEL

(japan)

Ahern, Michael – Production Coordinator
Allison, Mike – Sound Technician
Armstrong, Tom – Site Coordinator
Bakal, Gerry – Carpenter
Baptista, Joe – Site Coordinator
Beck, Dennis – Steel Team
Bender, Bob – Security
Berger, Bill – Carpenter
Brade, Rowan – Security
Brandhorst, David – Steel Team
Brant, Doug – Lighting Technician
Brockman, Tim – Promoter Security
Calderon, Tracy – Camera Operator
Callaghan, James – Security Chief
Campion, Edmund – Electrician
Campion, John – Master Electrician
Carter, Clay – Rigger
Caston, Monica – Video Camera Operator
Clements, Caroline – Makeup
Cofield, Michael – Pyro Technician
Cohl, Michael – Tour Director
Conyers, David – Sound Crew Chief
Cooke, Ystffan – Inflatables
Curtis, Lynn – Assistant to Norman Perry
Daltz, Bob – Promoter Production Coordinator
Daniel, Peter – Video Projectionist
DeBeauport, Pierre – Guitar Technician
Delahanty, Jim – Rigging Supervisor
Dunn, Alan – Logistics
Dunn, Arnold – Band Road Manager
Efron, Paul – Carpenter
Eike, Torje – Physiotherapist
England, Mark – Lighting Technician
Epstein, Gary – Sound Technician
Faris, Bryan – Lighting Technician
Ferrugia, Sam – Carpenter
Fisher, Mark – Set Design and Art Direction

Fleming, Mark – Steel Team
Fortune, Jay – Carpenter
Gilleland, Jerry – Tour Production Manager
Gnesin, Fern – Dressing Rooms
Goldman, Donna – Production Office Coordinator
Green, Colin – Lighting Technician
Greenberg, Robbie – Varilite Technician
Grenier, Bob – Rigging Supervisor
Griffin, Neal – Video Projectionist
Guinness, Miranda – Assistant to Mr. Jagger
Harbin, Eddie – Sound Technician
Hill, David – Lighting Director
Horgan, William – Security
Howard, Jo – Assistant to Mr. Wood
Howard, Steve – Promoter Production Manager
Huffman, Dan – Sound Technician
Jackson, Helena – Video Camera Operator
Jones, Nick – Merchandising
Kerr, Mike – Steel Team
King, Elizabeth – Lighting Technician
King, Tony – Press Liaison
Klvana, Cindy – Production Assistant
Kohorn, Mark – Carpenter
Lakota, Anne – Video Camera Operator
Lazar, Shelley – Administrative Assistant
Ledwith, Patrick – Steel Team
Lefevre, Benji – House Audio Engineer
Magee, Church – Band Crew Chief
McLeod, Robin – Video Camera Operator
Miller, Michael – Steel Crew
Muncrief, Lon – Steel Team
Newlin, Mark – Sound Technician
Ogilvie-Grant, Alex – Assistant Financial Controller
Oliver, Bea – Carpenter
Park, Jonathan – Set Design
Parker, Steve – Inflatables
Payne, Keith – Inflatables
Perry, Norman – Assistant Tour Director
Randel, Gary – Varilite Technician
Rels, Greg – Camera Engineer

Richardson, Bob – Carpenter
Rickards, Joel – Lighting Technician
Riggio, Jaye – Assistant to Michael Cohl
Robinson, Tom – Steel Team
Rongo, Steve – Carpenter
Russell, Tony – Assistant to Mr. Richards
Scovill, Scott – Video Projectionist
Seabrook, Joe – Security
Shepherd, Stephen – Drum Technician
Skidmore, Paul – Steel Team
Smith, Lavelle – Choreographer
Stallbaumer, David – Stage Manager
Stingel, George – Steel Team
Strand, Christine – Video Director
Sullivan, Jim – Merchandising
Sutherland, Angus – Guitar Technician
Tanzman, Linn – Press Representative
Thomas, Steve – Promoter Site Coordinator
Topeka, Andy – Keyboard Technician
Torffield, Marvin – On Air Projection
Townsend, Mary – Steel Team
Wade, Glenn – Panni Projectionist
Wade-Evans, Chris – Monitor Audio Engineer
Ward, Scott – Pyro Technician
Ward, Scott – Rigger
Wein, Bob – Promoter Security Director
Wetzell, Henry – Electrician
Wiesman, Michael – Lead Carpenter
Wille, Randy – Sound Technician
Williams, Fiona – Stylist
Wilson, Charlie – Lighting Crew Chief
Wolters, Rande – Rigger
Woodroffe, Patrick – Lighting Designer and Art Direction
Woolley, Timm – Financial Controller
Wynne, Joseph – Steel Team

Special thanks to the following for all their help

Academy Costume, Valerie Adamson, Hiroshi Akiyama, Azzedine Alaia, Lawrence Anderson, Mace Bailey, Sterling Ball, David Bernstien, Peter Berry, Trish Biggar, Jay Black, John Branca, Mike Brown, Cliff Burnstein, August Busch IV, Chris Chapman, Marianne Colaneri, Brian Collings, Chris Combs, Joe Corcoran, Brian Croft, Janice Crotch, Dave Crump, Sherry Daly, Don Dawson, Dennis Davis, Malcolm Doak, Patricia Dupont, Gene Evans, Fred Feingold, Ken Fitch, Arthur Fogel, Annie Fowler, Bob Franceschelli, Gary Geller, Marion Goddard, Paddy Grafton Green, Lee Griffin, Adrian Gwillyin, Mike Hawksworth, Jane Hayes, Rob Harries, Richard Hartman, Lydia Hernandez, Steve Howard, Walter Howell, Penelope Hyer, Lynette Jackson-Lammers, Karen Kearne, Carol Kelleher, Sally Anne Kenneally, Paige Kevan, Chris Kelly, Kenji Kitatami, Michael Kovine, Cynthia Klvana, Howard Kushner, Rhona Levene, Richard Leher, William Ivey Long, Rupert Lowenstein, Mike Lynch, Robin Magruder, Matt Masciandaro, Barbara Maters, Bob McCann, Tony McCuaig, Bill McNulty, Peter Mensch, Hubert Michard–Pellissier, Michiko, Bill Miller, Sue Millership, Barry Mindell, Paul Minter, Isaac Mizrahi, Keith Morley, Aiden Mullen, Andrew Murray, David Nutter, Tim Norman, Sieji Osaka, Joe Owens, Sam Parker, Peter Parcher, Tony Perry, John Piersce, Sandy Powell, Mr and Mrs Charles Pozzo, John Richmond, Derek Michael Roll, Jane Rose, Nancy Rosenblatt, Dominique Sallembien, Mathilde Sandberg, Stuart Samuels, Noela Sanderson, Jim Schobell, Tim Schoem, Marlene Schwartz, Alan Selzer, Jay Sendyk, Hisatake Shibuya, Tommy Shigetomi, Edwin Shirley, Brent Silver, Linda Simmons, Howard Siuclare, Randal Smith, Claire Stone, Kevin Tooley, Seijiro Udo, Frank van Hoorn, Debbie Walker, Guy Wallace, Jerome Walton, Andrew Wilkinson, Steve Winter, John Wohlegemuth, Jamie Wood, Leah Wood, Tyrone Wood, Julie Fusella Woolley, Chris Wright, Yasmin at Jones, Lance Yates.